Engaging the Soul of the Great Plains and the Smoky Hill Trail

by Carla M. Paton

HPP
HARD PAN PRESS

Dedication

Dedicated to my parents, Maurice Edward Pautz and Helen

Dorothy Kesler, and to their pioneering Prussian, German,

Scottish, and English forbearers: the Danfords, Clearys, and

Ramseys.

Table of Contents

Preface

This book explores the idea that natural and cultural places, such as the Great Plains and Smoky Hill Trail, have an archetypal coherence which can powerfully link us to our individual and collective depths. The scope of the study is the historical, natural, and cultural environment of the Great Plains area of the United States, and specifically the Smoky Hill Trail as depicted through its land, myth, and history. This method of analysis, which incorporates historical accounts, personal narrative essays, and fictional material, is situated in depth psychological ontologies, and terrapsychology inquiry methods as first proposed by Chalquist (2007). In addition, the work attempts to extend terrapsychology and depth psychology by locating correspondences between psyche and alchemy of Place. The conclusion drawn is that engagement and a psychic bond with the Great Plains is possible when a deep phenomenological exploration of Place is mapped which

assumes autonomy of soul.

"It is here that our hearts are set,

In the expanse of the heavens."

—Pawnee song

Beginnings

"It is no mere coincidence that our feelings about a place take on spiritual dimensions. An old rancher once told me he thought the lines in his hands had come directly up from the earth that the land had carved them there after so many years of work."

—Gretel Ehrlich, "Landscape"

With the aging of my parents, now in their eighties, and our joint purchase of a large tract of ranch land on the Eastern Colorado Plains, I feel them, myself, and my children, three generations, coming full circle. The prairies and plains of Western Kansas and Eastern Colorado have been our home and homeland for many generations.

Here, I hope to share some of this area's story, my family's story, as well as insight into why this particular place exerts such a powerful claim on me and others. My intention is to illustrate that place can link us to our individual and collective depths, as well as provide healing and transformation with the Earth, within ourselves, and communities. To do this, I will explore the archetype and cohesion of place—its alchemical synthesis of land, myth, and history—by focusing on one specific area: the Smoky Hill Trail as it traverses time and the plains of Kansas and Colorado.

My overall method is best reflected in the practice of *terrapsychology* that Chalquist (2012) developed for engaging the soul of place:

> Terrapsychology is the deep study of our largely unconscious (because disregarded) connections to and interdependencies with the multileveled presence of our living Earth, including specific places, creatures, and materials. "Deep" because what links us to places and animals and the elements travels along bridges of symbol, metaphor, image, and even synchronicity and dream. Terrapsychology explores how the patterns, shapes, features, and motifs at play in the nonhuman world sculpt our ideas, our habits, our relationships, culture, and sense of self: freeway congestion in congested conversations, lake toxins in our darker moods, salt-choked fields and bitter relations, healing landscapes and regenerating hearts. We also

study the reverse, the province of ecopsychology:
the impacts of colonialism, nationalism, and other
dissociative cultural constructs on the increasingly
paved and gridded world around us. (pp. 1-2)

Engaging the soul of a place also tugs on our
personal sense of home and an archetypal sense of innate
yearning for a place of our own. In finding and making our
home, it then becomes a sacred space. Since our desire for
and sense of land and home are remarkably similar in all
cultures throughout history, they also displays profound
archetypal energy. This archetypal field is strongly felt not
only in our designated home or sacred sense of place, but
also in nature and within cultural groups. In addition, I will
explore what a deep map of Place might look like when it
includes the unconscious and an alchemical understanding
of nature as it relates to psyche.

The concept of archetypal energy is grounded in a
depth psychological framework. To tease this apart, the

dictionary definition of an *archetype* is an original pattern or model from which all things of the same kind are copied or on which they are based; a model or first form; a prototype. However, in Jungian psychology, an archetype is a collectively inherited unconscious idea, or pattern of thought which is universally present in individual psyches (Archetype, n.d.).

Chalquist (2012) further tied this archetypal energy to the natural world: "Manifestations of human psychic life, including patterns, symbols, and metaphors, link to correlates and correspondences in the natural world across perpetually interactive fields and through complex systems. In other words, geological, geographical, ecological, meteorological, etc. forces are psychological forces too" (p. 3).

The place that has been my home and sacred space, and that continues to exert strongly felt archetypal forces, is the American "Heartland" of the Great Plains. For me, this journey of soul engagement specifically began in Kansas where my parents and I were born. Every summer I get invited to our family reunion in Kansas. I rarely go any more, but when I do, I am instantly immersed in the archetypal field of the hardy pioneer, the depression-era family farm, and the Mid-western Main Street. Perhaps this is not any one archetype, but anyone who has spent time in a small Kansas or Nebraska town will tell you that there is a coherence of being that comes into play. Why is this? For one thing, it is a difficult life. The earth is hard and unforgiving. The rain is fickle. The trains no longer stop at the local depots now dry-rotted and busy only with tumbleweeds patrons.

As I alluded, I have recently begun to re-engage my pioneer roots. I may not have my parents much longer and I stand to lose their many stories and connections to the prairie, and my personal, cultural, and historic ties to both land and people, if I do not record their stories soon. In addition, my husband and I have bought a home and ranch together with my parents on 70 acres of rolling prairie in Eastern Colorado. The intention, moreover, is to start a bison ranch and to be able to eventually fully subsist on the land. Syncronistically, running through these acres, in Elbert County, are the remnants of the "Smoky Hill Trail" that brought the pioneers in the 1850s to 1880s in covered wagons from Eastern Kansas towns to the gold fields of Denver, Colorado and Cherry Creek environs. My last suburban home, southeast of Denver, by Piney Creek, also lies along the Smoky Hill Trail. A plaque, commemorating the trail was a five-minute walk from that home (Figure 1).

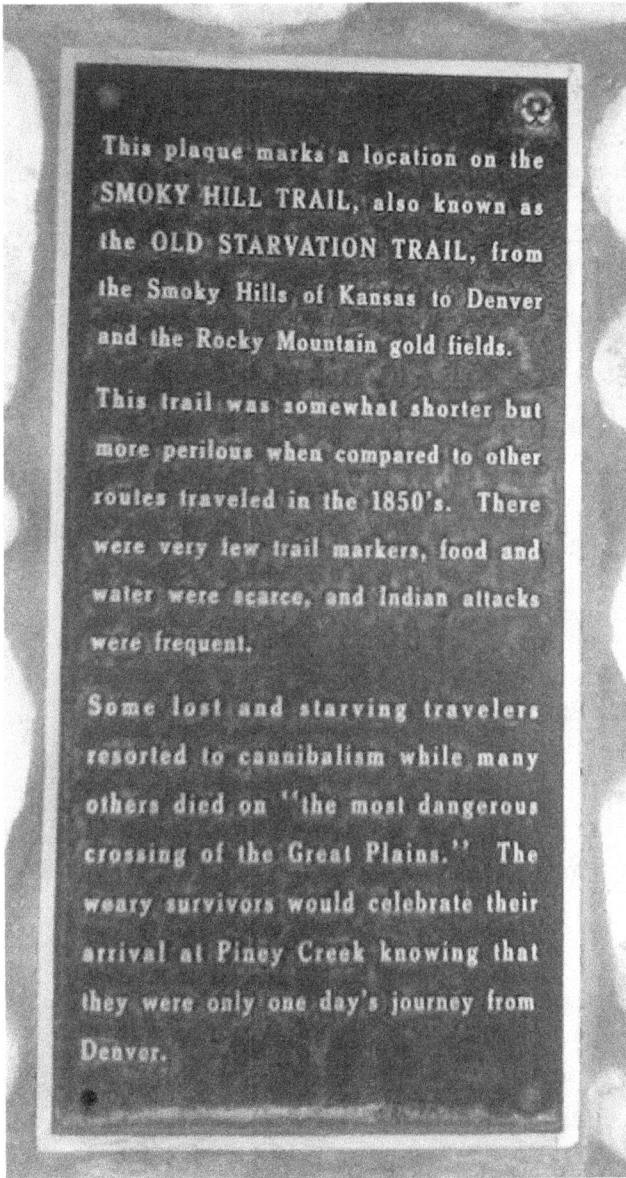

Figure 1. Piney Creek Smoky Hill Trail Marker, Centennial, Colorado © 2014
Carla Paton

Hillman (1983) maintained that soul-making, "Does not seek a way out of or beyond the world toward redemption or mystical transcendence…. The curative or salvational vision of archetypal psychology focuses upon the soul in the world which is also the soul of the world" (p. 26). It is by focusing on the earth, the world, what is underfoot and overhead that I find transformative. According to Edinger, (1985) in alchemy, this solidity is also known as *coagulatio:*

> 'Earth' is thus one of the synonyms for the *coagulatio.* It is heavy and permanent, of fixed position and shape… Its form and location are fixed. Thus, for a psychic content to become earth means that it has been concretized in a particular localized form; that is, *it has become attached to an ego.* (p. 83)

Indeed, our ego and our psyche live in the particulars of history, wind, storms, drought, rain, and dirt.

The "Old Starvation Trail" is in many ways representative of my "particular localized form" and engagement of the soul of the Great Plains. It stretches not only through the heart of my connections with the land of Kansas and Colorado, but it is a thread through time connecting the history of the earth, rivers, First Peoples, animals, pioneers, wagons, coaches, railroads, hope, destruction, and finally the modern highway covering over the foot, wagon, and rail tracks. Few who drive by the trail markers are aware of the history buried in layers under their wheels. My own deep desire for engagement with this place, its land, history, and myths moves me to discover how its voice articulates if we pause and sit awhile among the sea of grass.

A Great Expanse

"We could feel the peace and power of the Great Mystery

in the soft grass under our feet and in the blue sky above us.

All this made deep feeling within us, and this is how we got

our religion."

—Luther Standing Bear, *My Indian Boyhood*

My only memories of Kansas occur in the summer. This is because we drove our motorhome across the country from Maryland to Colorado during my father's three-week vacations. One would not attempt such a trek during the unpredictable winter months. In one such summer Kansas memory, my older brother, my father, and I sat watching "Lawrence Welk" on television, in the small farmhouse of an uncle. My mother and aunt were in the kitchen preparing supper (dinner, in the mid-west, is the word for lunch). My younger cousins seemed riveted by the show, but my brother rolled his eyes, which meant if he had to listen to one more singing duet with Mr. Welk he might go hang himself in the barn. I was more interested in my father. Every window was open and three floor fans were on full blast, yet my blouse clung to me from the humidity building with the late afternoon heat. My father ignored the television and was intent on looking out the large window. When he got up to smoke his pipe outside, I followed him.

I was unprepared for what I saw when I followed his gaze. Even as a meteorologist's daughter, I had never seen such foreboding black clouds. I have never forgotten it, or the electric feel to the air.

According to Heat, (1991) *tornado* is a Spanish word meaning turned, from a verb meaning to turn, alter, transform, repeat, and to *restore*. It is the tempest of opposing forces turning in, strengthening, as it gathers dry, cold air and mixes it with moist, warm air. This union of opposites, or alchemy of *coniunctio* that Edinger (1985) depicted; turns and whirls like star trails circling the poles, transmuting the air and the land wherever the opus, its work, converges to its most powerful culmination (p. 226). It is difficult to imagine how such a destructive work might restore anything, especially as restorative of psyche, unless we consider Jung's (1971) concept of the inferior-type function. In her 1971, *Lectures on Jung's Typology*, von Franz related that the inferior function has immense power due to the oppositional forces of consciousness (represented by the superior function) and the unconscious (represented by the inferior function). Also, according to Jung, (1959) "the inferior function is practically identical with the dark side of the human personality" (CW 9i, Para. 222). One might extend this to imagine the tornado as the shadow side of nature, the destructive energy necessary to balance the creative force.

I am especially conscious of the weather, no matter where I live or travel. My father trained as a meteorologist in the U.S. Air Force; at the University of Chicago under Dr. Fujita (designer of the tornado intensity "F-Scale" rating); at the Kansas Severe Storm Center and the National Weather Service in Washington D.C.; finally, he was the "Meteorologist In Charge" of the State of Colorado. Weather is deep in my psyche. Tornadoes especially frequent most of my dreams since tornadoes of every configuration covered my father's office walls. I am no "storm chaser" but I do get a thrill when the clouds start building. Many afternoons and evenings I sat huddled in a blanket watching the natural fireworks of lighting and my father's pipe smoke curling around his head. However, it was the sweet rain above all that we honored with unspoken reverence. A smell like no other; like wet jasmine in Maryland, and in Colorado, like parched dirt freshly washed; the scent of fragrant sheets on a clothes line.

On the Great Plains the vast open space contributes to spectacular weather patterns that add to the land's psyche and that of its inhabitants. Quantic (1997) in her book, *The Nature of Place: A Study of Great Plains Fiction*, spoke to this phenomenon of open space and weather:

> In a region where there are no natural barriers the
> great expanses exacerbate the weather's natural
> violence, and the land's products continue to
> influence the quality of life, no matter how far

removed one imagines oneself to be from the land. The drought, the coming storm, the promised crops are the stuff of daily newscasts and journalists' analyses. Social calendars, sporting plans, conversations, and jokes depend upon the weather and the nature of the land. (p. xii)

For many, the pioneers included, the Great Plains and prairie are a harsh, unforgiving land, severe weather or no. Also, many people, unaccustomed to miles of arid lands without trees, the stark beauty of the short and tall grasses, yucca, jackrabbits, and grasshoppers are lost on them. Europeans and Americans from the East, accustomed to deciduous forests, not only failed in transporting their water-reliant farming practices, but their psyches also found challenge in conforming to being dwarfed by the landscape. Cather's (1999) character, Alexandra Bergson (as well as Willa Cather herself) in *O Pioneers!* was

perhaps an exception in this clash of expectations and
reality:

> When the road began to climb the first long swells
>
> of the Divide, Alexandra hummed an old Swedish
>
> hymn, and Emil wondered why his sister looked so
>
> happy. Her face was so radiant that he felt shy about
>
> asking her. For the first time, perhaps, since that
>
> land emerged from the waters of geologic ages, a
>
> human face was set toward it with love and
>
> yearning. It seemed beautiful to her, rich and strong
>
> and glorious. Her eyes drank in the breadth of it,
>
> until her tears blinded her. Then the Genius of the
>
> Divide, the great, free spirit which breathes across
>
> it, must have bent lower than it ever bent to a
>
> human will before. The history of every country
>
> begins in the heart of a man or a woman. (p. 170)

One aspect of this land and weather that Quantic

spoke directly to, and to which Cather implied, is drought.

In the quote above, Alexandra views the land not from its drought aspect, but she sees it in the reverse. It is a land that "swells" and land that "emerged from the waters." There is moistness in her "love and yearning." Her eyes "drank" and blinded her with tears. The "great, free spirit" that could blow a drying wind, also "breathes" across the Divide. This is a moist breath as moist as the blood in the "heart of a man or a woman"—as moist as the blood that Alexandra works into the soil with her hands.

Collective Dreams

"Myths matter because they are the collective dreams that wed inner and outer, people and places, known and unknown. Myths image deep structurings of the human experience of the nonhuman."

—Craig Chalquist, *Terrapsychology: Re-engaging the Soul of Place*

"Grass no good upside down."

—Plains Indian admonition to white settlers

It is not only the land that can energize the field of a place; a *complex* can also generate a bundle of psychic energy "organized around a certain theme," which can be the magnetic pull, the "attractor," of archetypes on the individual and collective psyche (Conforti, 2003, p. 24). Conforti clarified that complexes act as "antennae" or "tuning mechanisms" for us to connect or not connect with certain archetypes and, specifically, certain traits or "frequencies" of particular archetypes (p. 24). Whitmont (1969) also said that "archetypes manifest indirectly as an archetypal image in a symbol, complex, or symptom" (p. 119). In America, the Great Dust Bowl brought together all the elements of nature, place, history and culture to create such a syndrome of complexes and symptoms that still shape the American psyche.

Whether it expresses itself through human art or nature, according to Portmann, "the mandate for virtually all-living systems...is twofold: to insure survival and to express one's nature" (cited in Conforti, 2003, p. xxv).

Indeed, Conforti added, "an *a priori* field, where form, living *in potentia*, is converted into matter" (p. xxvi). This "matter" can take many forms, not only in nature, but also in how we view nature and how we find our center, our home within this form. In turn, our imagination originates from this natural home center. And our imagination has Romantic roots.

Part of the European Romantic imagination that arrived on the shores of the New World along with the original settlers, as well as later Old World immigrants, was a longing for an "eternal return" to a pastoral lifestyle and ideal. This keenly felt sense of a lost Eden or natural, unspoiled landscape accompanied an escape from crowded, industrial, polluted European cities. When America's dense virginal forests, teeming wild life, wide open frontiers, and abundant natural resources were first learned of, it quickly translated into manifest destiny, the Homestead Act, the transcontinental railroad, the gold rush, and the primacy of progress (Marx, 1964). In their earnest desire to create a garden for themselves and their children, the settlers soon recreated cities, decimated indigenous peoples and species, and created vast dust bowls of over-cultivated topsoil.

This Edenic, pastoral archetypal ideal that we still persist in claiming as our birthright as Americans, continues to shape our cultural selective memory and therefore shapes our actions still. For example, instead of thinking logically of how to create dense population centers with minimal ecological impact, our longing for nature causes us to spread out our population centers, resulting in urban sprawl. By each of us desiring our little parcel of land, we have created thousands of suburbias with patches of thirsty lawns that require water and fertilizers in desert or semi-arid environments (Pollan, 1990). We have selective memory when it comes to soothing the wound of our *industrial complex*. In our effort to each grasp our own piece of nature, the collective; the land held in common is destroyed or altered, which recreates the wound in a vicious circle. Yes, our appreciation, our love of nature, or the cultivation of the love of nature may contribute to preserving it, but if our complex surrounding the pastoral archetype goes unrecognized, our love becomes smothering, consuming, and leads to a loss of the very thing so earnestly desired.

At the turn of the 19th century, the millions of virgin acres of the United States' Southern Plains called to pioneers. The black topsoil, rich as chocolate from long rain cycles, soon yielded record crops. The newly built railroads brought more farmers, eastern farming practices and soon wheat speculators. The horse and plow that plowed a mere three acres a day were replaced with tractors that could turn over fifty acres. Father and son took turns running the new shining green John Deeres night and day. Then, in the summer of 1931, the rains stopped. The drought continued for a decade. It took 1,000 years to make one inch of topsoil; in a few minutes of a dust storm, it was gone. The massively tall and wide black whirlwinds blotted out all light. For many, it appeared to be the end of the world (Worster, 2004).

It should be remembered that the word "soil" is also "humus," from which, etymologically, we also derive "humility" (Chevalier, 1996, p. 331). Jung (2002) also spoke to the hubris of ignoring the intrinsic qualities of the earth: "The facts of nature cannot in the long run be violated. Penetrating and seeping through everything like water, they will undermine any system that fails to take account of them, and sooner or later they will bring about its downfall" (p. 128).

Even as the dust storms and some of the hottest summers on record persisted, farmers continued to plow, believing that the rains would return and that the earth would still serve up its bounty once more. Many would internalize the outer event of the "Dust Bowl." The colossal clouds of darkness, mountains of dirt, ruined crops, constant grit in their food and teeth, choking and claustrophobia represented Western Kansas, the Depression and their childhood (my mother for one). This became their lens on the world; a world of constant worry, fear, hunger and lack. In turn, the following generation was molded by parents always preparing for the worst-case scenario, with the dust cloud always lurking on the horizon.

In alchemical terms, drought and dryness are associated with fire and the process of *calcinatio*. Edinger (1985) spoke of *calcinatio* as a drying-out process. "The necessary frustration of desirousness or concupiscence" is also a feature of this alchemical stage (p. 42). The dust bowl certainty frustrated many farmers and perhaps some in hindsight were able to "see the archetypal aspect of existence" (p. 44).

Following The Smoky Hill Trail

According to an early edition of Webster's Unabridged

Dictionary, the word 'Kansas' in the Indian vernacular

means "Smoky Water." This reference applies particularly

to the stream commonly known as the Smoky Hill.... The

Smoky Hill river is shown on early maps as the River of the

Padoucas, from the fact that the stream has its source in

territory occupied for ages by the Comanche Indians, or, as

they were first known, Padoucas.

—George Root, *Ferries in Kansas*

A few blocks from my previous home is a wondrous sight of equal opportunity for the dead—and the un-dead. A *Bed Bath and Beyond*, a *TGIF Fridays*, a *Chick-fil-A* restaurant, a four-lane highway, and of course in the middle of all, a 120-year-old pioneer cemetery enclosed with iron fencing and a five-pound padlock. I think the cemetery was there first.

There are little clues to this fifty-by-fifty-square-yard plot of silent history. The modern sign emblazoned atop the fencing proclaims it as the "Melvin-Lewis Cemetery." The prairie grass grows tall, it is impossible to see if any headstones remain. A new commemorative marker lies a few feet in from the fence, but the padlock makes it impossible to read without binoculars.

"The living" drive-by this peculiar shopping center attraction without a glance. It does not have a drive-through or double espressos. It does have the Colorado State Anatomical Board's registered remains of the 1,662 cremated souls who gave their earthly bodies to medical research. Many years after a few unregistered pioneers of the Pike's Peak gold rush made the ground their final home, the University of Colorado and Health Sciences Center bought the land and decided it was a nice spot for a few more bodies (Crowle, 2004).

The pioneers, Melvin and Lewis, who gave their name to the cemetery, also created the small community of Melvin, Colorado. The cemetery overlooked Melvin until the houses and buildings were condemned and submerged under Cherry Creek Reservoir, created by damming Cherry Creek in 1950. Melvin or Melvin City, as it was also known, began as "12-Mile House" (*Piney Creek History*, 2012).

From the 1850s to the 1880s, entrepreneurial ranchers and farmers erected stagecoach stops along the Butterfield Overland Dispatch, which followed the Smoky Hill Trail, about every four miles along Cherry Creek, from the present day Parker, Colorado to the terminus of the Smoky Hill Trail in Denver. The owners of the "mile houses," like John Melvin, provided fresh mules or horse teams, meals, lodging, and goods to weary gold seekers who had made the dangerous trek from Leavenworth, Kansas and other locales of eastern civil society (Lee, 1980). If they survived the frequent Indian attacks, broken wagons, starvation, or cannibalism of the "Starvation Trail," they could enjoy the region's then-largest hotel, which John and his wife Jane built at Melvin. After the hotel, John and others added a tavern, post office, and a half-mile racetrack, all now tranquilly rotting under the water of Cherry Creek Reservoir.

I know that some parts of Melvin still linger by the ancient cottonwoods that have survived the years and water invasion. As I walk the trails around the reservoir, now a State Park, I wander off the worn path and seek out the shade where I know John and Jane once sat. A few broken stone foundations speak from the dirt far from anyone's

notice except those seeking wagon wheel ruts and shadows.

Connections

Grass is the most widely distributed of all vegetable beings

and is at once the type of our life and the emblem of our

mortality...the carpet of the infant becomes the blanket of

the dead.

—John James Ingalls, *In Praise of Blue Grass*

Although there has been a successful effort in Kansas to mark the Smoky Hill Trail and the Butterfield Overland Dispatch, this has not been the case in Colorado. Little remains of the trail except for a few plaques, a road called "Smoky Hill Road," and the name of a high school (which my children attended). I would venture that most residents near the road or high school have no knowledge of the Smoky Hill River (which originates much further east) or the long history of its namesake's trail.

Likewise, the majority of descendants of the Great Plains pioneers have moved to large cities, forgetting or never knowing their cultural heritage. With this forgetting, comes a loss of connection to the land and place that shaped the psyche of its inhabitants and engaged the soul of the place. If we lose this connection to the open prairie, we stand to lose our open-heartedness and the wide spaces where psyche can move and breathe freely in boundless expanse of sky and ground. Jones (2000) echoed this archetypal power of place:

> We are part of the prairie; it is part of us. We inhale moisture given off by the transpiring grasses and breathe the oxygen they create during photosynthesis. We eat the seeds of the wheat, barley, and rye, and the roots of the other prairie plants. Our blood flows with the same molecules that nourish the big bluestem and cottonwood. Our collective memories radiate from the dusty savannas of central Africa and converge on the blood-soaked plains of the American West...Should we destroy what remains, we will lose much more than Indian grass, black-footed ferrets, burrowing owls, and grasshopper sparrows. We will lose an irreplaceable work of creation, a critical strand in the web of life that binds us to this planet and keeps our humanity

and spirit whole. We may, in Sweet Medicine's words, "become worse than crazy." (pp. 154-155)

Edinger (1985) also related that, like the open plains, "the *prima materia* is undifferentiated, without definite boundaries, limits, or form. This corresponds to a certain experience of the unconscious that exposes the ego to the infinite, the *apeiron*" (p. 12).

When my parents are gone, I know I may be one of the last generation to feel "part of the prairie" and it part of me. Still, I am bringing my children out to the Eastern Colorado plains soon. We hope to bring some buffalo back to the land; we hope to see the stars. I hope we can, for a time, sit out on the back porch, with my father, and watch the billowing sky signs. Perhaps I will one day hold a grandbaby on my hip and tell them about the nearby pioneer trail. We can get down on our hands and knees to feel the native grasses that have tough roots that grow deep into the heart of the land.

References

Archetype. (n.d.). In *Dictionary.com*. Retrieved July 27, 2012, from http://dictionary.reference.com/browse/archetype?s =t

Cather, W. (1999). *Novels & Stories, 1905-1918*. New York: College Editions.

Chalquist, C., & Gomes, M. E. (2007). *Terrapsychology: Re-engaging the Soul of Place*. New Orleans: Spring Journal Books.

Chalquist, C. (2012). "TI2: An Integrative Methodology for Coming Home to Place, Nature, Matter, and Earth". Retrieved July 27, 2012, from TerraPsych.com, http://www.terrapsych.com/

Chevalier, J., & Gheerbrant, A. (1996). *The Penguin Dictionary of Symbols*. London: Penguin.

Conforti, M. (2003). *Field, Form and Fate*. New Orleans,

LA: Spring Journal Books.

Crowle, C. (2004). *CCHVS: History*. Retrieved July 27,

2012, from

http://www.cherrycreekvalleyhistoricalsociety.org/h

istory.htm

Edinger, E. F. (1985). *Anatomy of the Psyche: Alchemical

Symbolism in Psychotherapy*. La Salle, Ill: Open

Court.

Ehrlich, G. (2002). "Landscape". In L. Anderson, & T.S.

Edwards, *At Home on This Earth: Two Centuries of

U.S. Women's Nature Writing* (p. 307). Hanover,

NH: University Press of New England.

Heat, M. W. L. (1991). *PrairyErth: (A Deep Map)*. Boston:

Houghton Mifflin.

Hillman, J. (1983). *Archetypal Psychology: A Brief Account*. Dallas: Spring Publications.

Ingalls, J. J. "In Praise of Blue Grass". Retrieved July 27, 2012, from http://naldc.nal.usda.gov/download/IND43894989/P DF

Jones, S. R. (2006). *The Last Prairie: A Sandhills Journal*. Lincoln: University of Nebraska Press.

Jung, C. G. (1971). "A Psychological Theory of Types" (R.F.C. Hull, Trans.). In H. Read et al. (Series Eds.), *The Collected Works of C.G. Jung* (Vol. 6). Princeton, NJ: Princeton University Press.

_____., & Hull, R. F. C. (1959). *Collected Works of C.G. Jung/ [Vol. 9, part 1] The Archetypes and the Collective Unconscious*. New York, N.Y: Pantheon Books.

_____., & Sabini, M. (2002). *The Earth Has a Soul: The Nature Writings of C.G. Jung*. Berkeley, Calif: North Atlantic Books.

Lee, W. C., & Raynesford, H. C. (1980). *Trails of the Smoky Hill: From Coronado to the Cow Towns*. Caldwell, Idaho: Caxton Printers.

Marx, L. (1964). *The Machine in the Garden: Technology and the Pastoral Ideal in America*. New York: Oxford University Press.

Piney Creek History. (2012). Retrieved July 27, 2012, http://www.pineycreek.org/info.php?pnum=15

Pollan, M. (1990). Why mow? The case against lawns. In S. H. Slovic, & T. F. Dixon, *Being in the world: An Environmental Reader for Writers* (pp. 433-443). New York, New York: Macmillan Publishing Company.

Quantic, D. D. (1997). *The Nature of the Place: A Study of Great Plains Fiction*. Lincoln: University of Nebraska Press.

Root, G. A. (1935). *"Ferries in Kansas, Part VI — Smoky Hill River"*. Retrieved July 29, 2012, http://www.kancoll.org/khq/1935/35_1_root.htm

von Franz, M. L. & Hillman, J. (1971). *Lectures on Jung's Typology*. Dallas, TX: Spring Publications.

Whitmont, E. C., & C.G. Jung Foundation for Analytical Psychology. (1969). *The Symbolic Quest: Basic Concepts of Analytical Psychology*. New York: Published by Putnam for the C.G. Jung Foundation for Analytical Psychology.

Worster, D. (2004). *Dust Bowl: The Southern Plains in the 1930s*. Oxford: Oxford University Press.